ED / EN

**GOD'S DREAM
FOR THE WORLD**

JOSHUA SHAW

EDEN: God's Dream for the World
© 2018 by Joshua Shaw

EDEN: God's Dream for the World by Joshua Shaw
Published by Lighthouse Church // Books
8210 W. 10th Ave, Lakewood, CO 80214
www.lighthousechurch.tv

Unless otherwise indicated, Scripture quotations are from The Holy Bible, New International Version®, NIV. Copyright © 1973, 1978, 1984, by Biblica, Inc.™ Used by Permission. All rights reserved worldwide.

Although the men and women whose stories are told in this book are real, many of their names have been changed to protect their privacy.

Where italics occur within scripture quotes, emphasis has been added by the author.

Cover Design and Page Layout by Joshua Shaw.

ISBN-13: 978-1718090071 (Lighthouse Books)

While the author has made every effort to provide accurate Internet addresses at the time of publication, neither the publisher nor the author assumes any responsibility for errors or for changes that occur after publication.

Printed in the United States of America

Acknowledgments

One of my greatest passions in life has been to be a writer. Well... actually to be a movie writer and director. But writer will have to do...

I have always wanted to be a writer, and as I came to know Jesus Christ, my passions turned towards writing for HIM. I always wanted to write to love my Savior. Almost like a young boy writes to his crush—I wanted to show Jesus just how *thankful* I was for him! (I know, I know, that image-ray is a bit weird. I am *not* dating Jesus, but I think you get the point).

As I have written this book—knowing it would be hard, knowing I would struggle with doubts and anxiety—I am forever grateful for my wife, Brianne, for Ryan (my co-pastor and editor), and for the many people at Lighthouse Church who encouraged me along the way.

You are all so precious to me.

Thank you!

Table of Contents

This book is gratefully written for:

Brianne - Thank you for your ever-present encouragement and love!

Zeke & Ash - My dudes—I love you both so much.

Lighthouse Church - I pray this gives you a new perspective on God's love for you.

...

A Message Our World Needs To Hear

God looked over at everything he had made; it was so good, so very good!

GENESIS 1:31 MSG

That Sucks!

"What on earth are you talking about?" That is the response Jeremy had as he was sitting across from me in our favorite coffee shop.

Every couple of months we would get together to catch up on life. Jeremy is not a Christian. He would claim that he's agnostic towards religion. In fact, if he was being really honest, his agnosticism is not because of well thought arguments. It's simply because he doesn't care.

He's never experienced God. He's never seen God in action. For him, agnosticism is out of priorities. There are too many other things that more than God so why bother? I am sure some of you can relate.

So there we were, drinking our coffee, talking about life, when the conversation turned to something more serious.

Like most guys I know, Jeremy didn't come out and say exactly what was on his mind. Guys typically don't do that. But as his coffee got to a re-fill point he said to me, "So... things aren't going well".

He didn't know how to initiate the conversation, but he knew he needed to.

"Things aren't going well."

Now, because I have worked in ministry for quite a while, I've learned the tricks of "heavy-conversation trade." I know when someone wants me to ask questions. I know when someone is looking for advice. I know when someone needs a shoulder to cry on. It's something that comes with the territory of working for a church. So when he began with those words I knew what to say next.

"What do you mean 'things aren't going well?'"

I restated his comment in the form of question to give him a chance to verbalize his thoughts a bit more., and as soon as I did that, flood-gates of information began to pour out.

||||||||

"Sarah and I are not doing well at all." He started.

"We've been trying to get pregnant for the past three years and nothing! I can't believe that we can't get pregnant. We're good people. We take care of our bodies. But nothing.

"My boss is getting on me for wanting to take more time to visit my dad who's dying of MS. I never had a good relationship with him, but I can't let him die without restoring our relationship. I have to care for him when he needs me the most. It's so hard. Do I get fire or care for my dad?

"Then there's this stuff about my health that I'm struggling with. The doctors have no idea why I'm losing weight. Sometimes I'm freaked out that I have

MS like my dad. Sometimes I think Sarah and I can't have a baby because I have a disease. Things just aren't going well, Josh, and I'm miserable."

| | | | | |

He poured his heart out to me, and to be honest, I wasn't ready for it. He had never said anything like this before. It was all new information to me. So I did what any normal person would do in that moment. I said, "Dang bro, that sucks."

So much for wise pastoral wisdom, right?

"That sucks."

It's all I could think of. I knew I was supposed to say something encouraging, but I couldn't. All I could say was what I was feeling in that moment.

"That sucks."

As I said those words, something unexpected occurred. I heard Jesus speak to Jeremy as well.

"Josh," Jesus began.

"Tell him that I think the same thing. Tell him that I didn't want this to happen. Tell him that I will fix everything. Tell him that I am with him. Tell him."

||||||

Now here's the deal. Before you think that I am some sort of super-Christian who has the Holy Spirit on speed dial, or that I have voices in my head, let me assure, I am *not* the type of person this happens to often. I don't hear Jesus' "still small voice" when I wake in the morning. I don't hear Jesus when I write my sermons on Thursday afternoons, and I certainly don't hear Jesus when I am in the middle of saying things like "that sucks" to my friends. It's not how God gifted me. But this time was different.

During this conversation Jesus decided to tell me what to say, and the words he shared with me were very specific. I was to tell Jeremy that he was not alone. That Jesus cared. And that his circumstances were not what God intended.

Now, let me ask you this. Do you think what I heard from Jesus was true?[1] Do you believe that Jesus understood Jeremy's pain? Do you believe that Jeremy was not alone? Do you believe that Jesus cared? Or perhaps most challenging, do you believe that what Jeremy was going through was _not_ what God wanted? That last question is a tricky one. Can Jesus be sovereign over everything _and_ allow for things to occur that break his heart?

Maybe, maybe not. But that's what I told Jeremy.

It Was All Very Good

"I know this may sound super strange, but God feels the same way you do. He doesn't want these things for you. In fact, what you are going through is the exact opposite of what he wants for you."

In response, well, let's just say he didn't know how to respond.

In all our years of friendship, I never said anything remotely close to this. Our conversations were usually about good restaurants in the city, our marriages, and working out. This was the first time we ever talked about something so spiritual. And in response, he sat sat there in silence.

After two minutes he looked up and said, "What on earth are you talking about? There is no way God cares about me. There is no way!"

I was not ready for his response.

More often than not, Jeremy is easy-going. It takes a lot to get him upset. But in this conversation, he was livid. He couldn't believe that God cared about him. He couldn't believe that God had a dream for his life. He couldn't believe it. So he challenged me.

"Everyone knows that God hates this world, Josh! He doesn't care about us. His whole goal is to burn everything up and start over anyways. So don't lie to me. I can't handle that right now."

Ouch!

I was in shock. And the entire time he yelled at me, claim that God didn't care, that God was going to start over anyways, I thought, "Is he wrong?"

I wasn't sure.

For thousands of years Christians have held a view of the world that isn't too optimistic. Almost all of our art has clouds, angels, and heaven painted with lush colors, and any time there is a reference to the world, it always seems to contain flames, judgement, and dark colors.

Some of our most famous books are about how Jesus is going to take us away from this wretched world and start over in heaven.[2]

Did you know that God's intention for every human on earth is to flourish and live an eternal life in blissful glory?

Was he wrong to say that God didn't care?

I wasn't sure, and once againJesus began to speak to me.

||||||

"It was all very good."

"What?"

"It was all very good, Josh."

Jesus was quoting Genesis 1:31 to me. He was quoting a passage of scripture that talks about the moment God looked at the created world called Eden, and while he looked at it all, he said, "It was all very good!"

In a moment when I had a friend crying out to me because he had lost all hope in life, Jesus reminded me of how wrong we both were.

"It was all very good!" (Gen. 1:31)

The Good (Unbelievable) News.

After Jesus reminded me of this passage, I began to show Jeremy God's dream for him from the Bible. I showed him passages of Scripture that proved that God never intended for people to suffer. I flipped to Old Testament stories that proved that God never wanted our world to be a place of sorrow. I told him that when God said "It was very good," in Genesis 1, he was proving to us that his dream for our world was the Garden of Eden, not the world as we know it to be. And in this Garden of Eden, God lived with humanity. There was no such thing as brokenness. There was no such thing as death. There was no such thing as hopeless. There was only eternal flourishing. And it has been God's dream, ever since the Fall, to *bring us back* to Eden through the power of Jesus Christ.

||||||

I shared this news with Jeremy, and by the time I was done, I realized that Jeremy wasn't the only person I knew that needed to hear it. He isn't the only person who thinks negatively about our world, and our suffering, and God's hand in all of it. He isn't the only person who needs to be told of God's dream of Eden and his promise to bring us back there.

Many of us don't know this news of Eden..

We have no idea that God's dream has always been for the world to "be good." We have no idea that when sorrow, and pain, and suffering, and loss, came into our world it was *not* what God wanted, and he has done *everything* necessary to fix was was once broken. We have no idea, or perhaps, we have too easily forgotten. Which is why I have written this book.

The Plan for this Book

In part one, I will paint a picture of God's dream for the world rooted Genesis 1-2. From there, I will discuss how God's dream went from being realized in Eden to something that we messed up in the fall, which required God to come up with a plan of restoration. During the second section of part one, we will dive into what God's plan was in restoring Eden and how throughout the Old Testament, God garden imagery to remind us that Eden was always his dream.

In part two, I will take the garden imagery that God used throughout the Old Testament and show how through life, death, and resurrection of Jesus, those gardens are fulfilled. Throughout the stories of Jesus found in the New Testament, Jesus systematically restores Eden. And in a moment of climactic bliss, in the final chapter, we will see how God's dream for our world changes every area of our lives.

I pray that as you join this story, just as Jeremy did, you would gain a new perspective, not only of Jesus and the Bible, but on God and his incredible dream for _you_ and _your life_.

Notes:

1 You will discover throughout this book that I am, along with our church, theologically charismatic. We believe in all the gifts of the Spirit, including the gift of prophecy. So if things like this bother you, think about them as informed promptings of the Holy Spirit that coincide with the teachings of the Bible.

2 See, Left Behind book series. Actually don't. They are mediocre fiction with terrible theology.

Part I: God's Dream

God's Dream of Eden

Every great dream begins with a dreamer.

HARRIET TUBMAN

I Have a Dream

On August 28th, 1963, Dr. Martin Luther King Jr. gave one of the greatest speeches in human history, "I Have a Dream." On this day, thousands of people swarmed Washington, D.C. to the footsteps of the Lincoln memorial where they listened with great anticipation as Dr. King dreamed with them.

In the midst of our country fighting against each other over issues of freedom and equality, Dr. King dreamed with his audience. He dreamed of a day when his sons and daughters were evaluated on their passions and abilities, rather than the color of their skin. He dreamed of a time in our country when his friends could achieve the American Dream without having to experience prejudice. He dreamed of a day when every person on earth would thrive and experience the prosperity of God, no matter where they were born, what language they spoke, or what shade their skin was.

He dreamed. And when he did, millions of people were inspired.

Even though they knew what Dr. King envisioned was not a reality yet, they were filled with hope. They were encouraged to see the world different. They were encouraged to dream on their own. And through their inspiration, systemic changes were made.

Dreams became a reality.

Dreams Are Powerful

Dreams are some of the most powerful tools of creation in our entire world. The act of imagining something that has yet to be created, stepping towards an unknown to see it come to completion is powerful.

It's world changing.

That's why Dr. King's speech was world-changing. He took the imaginations of millions of people on a dream-journey, and when it concluded, they couldn't help but jump onboard.

Dreams are powerful.

Now, as I say that, you may think that I am putting too much stock into dreams. Perhaps throughout your entire life you've been discouraged of dreaming, and you put more merit into "working hard."[1] Maybe you believe that dreaming is only for the young (and perhaps naive). But the reality is that every movement in the history of our world—for good and for evil—occurred because of a dream.

Think about one of the worst massacres in human history, the Holocaust. Six million Jews were slaughtered at the hands of Adolf Hitler, not because he didn't like Jews, but because he had a dream—a dream that, unfortunately, millions of other people bought into.

He dreamed of a world where only certain people who looked a certain way and adhered to a certain worldview could live. He dreamed of a world and as he dreamed, the world was changed forever.

||||||||

Think about America. A utopian democracy where people are free to pursue their own dreams, fight for their freedom, earn a living, and not have totalitarian leader demand allegiance from them. Do you think our society was born out of logical progressivism and hard work? I don't think so.

It was caused because of a dream—a dream of freedom. A dream of hope. A dream of prosperity influenced by the revelation of God himself.

> We hold these truths to be self-evident: that all men are created equal; that they are endowed by their Creator with certain unalienable rights; that among these are life, liberty, and the pursuit of happiness.

||||||

Think about your own life for a moment. Consider the most significant thing that has happened to you in recent memory. Maybe it's when your first child was born, or when you bought your first house, or when you traveled the Europe on a backpack trip after college, or when you landed that dream job.

How often did you dream about that before it happened? Years? Months? Days? It really doesn't matter how long you dreamed of it. The fact is that you *did* dream of it. You spent meaningful

> *God isn't having a conversation with Jesus and the Holy Spirit at a low enough volume to keep us guessing about the plans of heaven.*

time thinking about it, planning for it, and making it happen. And in the end, something life-changing occurred.

Dreams are powerful.

God Dreams, Too

Did you know that God dreams, too? It's an odd thing to think about because we don't like to put attributes of humanity on God. But the reality is that God dreams.

God dreams just like you and me, and the only difference between us and God when it comes to dreams is that *everything* God dreams becomes reality. In theological circles, we call these dreams his *will*, or his *plans*, or his *purposes*. God's dreams.

Just like Dr. King. Just like you and me. God dreams. And his dreams are always *positive*.

You see, anytime I talk with someone about their suffering, whether it be a lost job or a struggle with depression or whatever their suffering may be, they tend to spin it in a way that puts the blame on God.

"This must be God teaching me something."

"God must have thought that job was too good for me."

"God took that person from it because he knew I'd love them too much."

We spin the negative things of our lives to make it sound like God's dreams are always *against* our dream.

But what if I told you that that type of thinking was completely flawed? What if I were to *prove* to you that God's dreams for you are not negative but they are overwhelmingly positive—that he is for you, that he loves you, and he is plans are always good?

That would be amazing, wouldn't it?

Listening to the Conversation

When I was growing up, on a regular basis my parents had friends over for dinner. My mom and dad are excellent cooks and wonderful hosts, and because of that, people loved to be in our home for dinner.

During these dinners my parents had expectations on us kids. While they talked with their friends about life and work and we were expected listen to the conversation and add to it as appropriate. We were never kept from engaging the adults, but we were taught to be respectful and to ensure that our guests felt welcomed, rather than overwhelmed by a bunch of kids.

One of the things that I remember the most at these dinners is that when the meal was finished and the post-meal decaf coffee came out, that was our cue to head to bed. We had enjoyed our time with the adults, but it was time for us to go to sleep so that they could enjoy the rest of their evening alone.

Now, the reason why I remember this time of the evening more than anything else is because I suffer from a chronic disease called FOMO (Fear Of Missing Out). I can't handle when a party is happening without me. So, when I was too young to stay up with the adults, when we were sent off to our rooms, I would sit by my door, with my light turned off and my door cracked up just enough to listen to the conversations.

I did everything I could to listen in because I didn't want to be left out.

|||||||

Many of us have this type of mindset when we think about God's dreams. We think that every once and a while we are allow to sit at the table with God and hear conversations about life. God talks about what the angels are up to over the next millennia, and what heaven looks like, and a few other topics, but as soon as he gets to the good stuff—the stuff dreams are made of—it's time to go to bed. We are relegated to the bedroom so that the "adults" can talk and we miss out.

There is a huge problem with this type of thinking. *It's completely wrong.* God isn't sitting at the dining table of divinity with Jesus and the Holy Spirit talking at a low enough volume to keep us guessing about his dreams. Instead, he has fully disclosed his dreams for us to see.

From the very beginning of the Bible, in the book of Genesis, we are shown God's dream for the world. In those verses are shown something absolutely incredible. We are shown a garden. A beautiful. Perfect. Flourishing garden. One like we have never seen before.

In this garden, called the Garden of Eden, the world is perfect. There is no violence. There is no poverty. There is no death. There is only perfect, utopian peace.

In this garden every single human lives in harmony. There is no such thing as a marital disagreement or broken friendship. There is only peace.

In this garden there is no shame. There is no sexual pain. There is only innocence, purity, and satisfaction.

In this garden _purpose_ is given to every person. We are given a purpose and destiny.

In this garden there is no such thing as a dead end job. There is no such thing as a person who is a waste of space. Every man and woman is created by God to flourish, to care for what he provides, and to reign over it as good gardeners.

This is the Garden of Eden. But it doesn't stop there.

Eden doesn't just represent _peace_ and _purpose_, and _prosperity,_ but it represents God's _presence._

> _Eden, at least when I picture it, is like San Diego weather, meets Japanese food culture, meets Canadian kindness..._

God's dream is to be *present* for all humanity. He has no desire to be distant, forgotten, or rejected. But he has a dream to be *near*.

Have you ever cried out to God in the midst of a difficult situation and asked that he be near to you? Have you ever been at a point in your sorrow that no other person would satisfy—not a friend, a spouse, a parents—but only God?

In God's dream you never have to cry out to him because he is always near. Like a cool breeze on a perfect spring day, God near to you. Providing for you. Loving you.

Peace. Purpose. Prosperity. Presence.

That sounds perfect, doesn't it?

The Question

So, if this is God's dream for the world why do we live as if its not true? Why do we live thinking God couldn't care less about us? Why do we live like he is distant, like our sicknesses, struggles, and hardships are all *part* of his dreams?

Because we believe the lie that God's dream is way too good to be true.

|| |||||

You see, reason you think what I just described is way too good to be true is because you've been lied to for a long time. Allow me to explain.

If you grew up in the church I can guarantee you you heard sermons telling you that God was fed up with our world. That God was sick and tired of the sinfulness of humanity and one day he would burn everything up and start over.

Even if you didn't grow up in the church, I bet through random people at work or in school or through different Christian books you came to assume that God hates our world and hates you, and that he can't wait to start over with a new group of faithful religious people who persevere until the end.

Am I right?

Here's the deal, friend. That is all a lie.

The True Dream

God's dream has *always* been to create what we see in Genesis 1-3, the Garden of Eden. He has always dreamed of what your life could be like in Eden. He has always desired for our earth to look like a flourishing garden.

It has always been his ideal.

Even in the midst of his judgement he has always had his dream of Eden. Even in the midst of our rebellion, he has always had his dream of Eden. He has always dreamed of created a place where we flourish in his presence, where everything we do has purpose, where there is no pain, sorrow, or death. That is the dream of God.

And just like Dr. King, God stood atop the platform of the cosmos in Genesis 1, looking into the hopeful eyes of humanity, and he declared the greatest "I Have a Dream" speech in history:

"I have a dream. Where one day my children, and their children's children will never experience sorrow. Where my friends live in perfect peace together. Where no one ever questions their purpose or calling in life, but they would flourish.

"I have a dream where death ceases to exist. Where cancer has no place. Where tears only come out of the joy of laughter. Where spouses serve and love each other just as I serve and love my world.

"I have a dream where violence will not even be in the vocabulary of my creation, but peace with reign supreme.

"I have a dream. And *you* have a part to play in it."

Notes:

1 This is actually a bi-product of the "Builder" and "Boomer" generations. Due to the World Wars, creativity and ingenuity was stifled generationally. In fact, many sociologists attribute mid-life crises to the fact that, generationally speaking, they were not encouraged nor did they have the sociological ability to dream. As a result, dissatisfaction set in as they got older in life and "looked back" on their accomplishments.

3

God's Plan to Redeem Eden

I'm always sad to leave paradise, but I leave behind the hopes of coming again soon.

IRINA SHAYK

Tabor Walks

When I was in my early twenties I went to a small college called Tabor College. It was your stereotypical small-town Christian college where everything revolved around sports, chapel, and getting a "ring by spring."

One of the things that our campus was infamous for was what is called Tabor Walks. Tabor Walks were two hour escapades with newly developed romantic relationships, where couples walked around the campus, kissed behind the music building, and talked about the busy life of being at a college of 500 students.

In my first two years at Tabor I didn't have the priviledge of going on many of these walks. I was a city-boy who didn't fit into the culture of the midwest. I didn't speak the midwest

> *So after about nine failed attempts at asking her out for a date, we eventually became a couple, and let me tell you, we had plenty of Tabor walks.*

language. I didn't have the right last name. My approach to my faith was a bit different than most other people, which meant that Tabor Walks weren't really an option for me.

I guess I could have went on one all by myself, but who would want to walk around a college campus kissing an imaginary girlfriend? I wouldn't.

So, for my first two years, I didn't go on any Tabor Walks. But all of that changed when I met Brianne.

Brianne Nichole Greene was this beautiful, godly young woman that caught my eye. She was a Denver

Bronco fan, a connoisseur of Chipotle Burritos (the 4th member of the Trinity, by the way), and she was gorgeous. She was everything I had hoped for in a potential Tabor Walk partner.

After nine failed attempts at asking her out(yes, you read that correctly, nine attempts!), we eventually became a couple. And let me tell you, we had plenty of Tabor Walks.

On an almost nightly basis would spend hours walking around the campus dreaming about what God had in store for us. We dreamed of getting married, starting a church, and raising a family. It was a blissful season in both of our lives. A lot of our fondest memories go back to the times in the spring when we would walk in the cool of the afternoon dreaming together.

Walking with God

When God dreamed of Eden one of the most profound aspect of his dream is his desire to be *present* with humanity. In Genesis 3:8, we are told that when God created Adam and Eve, he would spend time with them in the "cool of the day."[1]

This is significant because when the book of Genesis was written, about 4,000 years ago, would have never described their god doing something like this. Gods didn't dwell with there people back then. But rather, they lived in heavenly throne rooms (think of Greek or Roman pantheons), and they superimposed their wills on humans. The thought of a god—the God who created the cosmos—dwelling with humanity would have sounded crazy. And yet, that is what God tells us is his dream for the world—to be with us, to dwell among us, to walk among us.

So what happened?

We Turned Away

The saddest moment in history is the moment humanity turned away. We had everything—life with God, purpose, peace—and yet, in our brokenness, we turned away. We took the God's dream and abandoned it for something we thought would be much greater.

This moment is called the Fall. It is the moment in history that we chose our dreams over God's dream. We chose ourselves over God. And when that happened, we lost everything.

In Genesis 3, we are told that after the fall, Adam and Eve were confronted by God about their infidelity and when they do that, everything starts to fall apart. They lie to God. They try to cheat their way out of their decisions. They fight against each other. They blame the serpent who deceived them. They do everything in their power to *reverse* their rebellion. But it's too late. They turned away, and a moment of heartbreak, God banishes them from the garden.

The Heart of God

I want you to put yourself into the shoes of God for a moment. So often when we study Genesis 3 we talk about Adam and Eve and focus on their deception, or the serpent, and we have massive debates about the "curses" that God warns them about, but I want you to focus on God for a moment.

For trillions of years God dreamed of a day when he would create a utopian world for humanity to experience with him. He breathed into existence the universe, starting with galaxies. He drew billions upon billions of galaxies, with billions upon billions of stars in them. Then he formed our solar system. He formed the sun and the earth. And he filled the earth with water, and mountains, and animals—all for your joy.

Then he created us. Like the infamous Bob Ross he look at the world he just created, and said, "Let's add some happy people in there." He formed each and every one of

> _If you think about it, Genesis 3 is a symbolic reminder that we had something incredible, something perfect, but we squandered it._

us, giving us personalities, dreams, and passions, all so that we could enjoy the Garden of Eden that he created.

Imagine the determination that took. Imagine the precision that took. Imagine the _love_ that took.

A garden is an amazing description of God's handiwork, isn't it? Toiling, striving, planning, preparing, all with the hopes of something beautiful coming from it.

And then, in a flash of a moment, it's all ruined.

The people he created to enjoy his dream destroy it because they want something better.

||||||

Imagine you had a 50,000 piece puzzle that you spent weeks working on. When you finished the puzzle you invited your best friend to come over to check it out. When they get to your house and look at the they throw it on the ground, shattering it to pieces. In an act of envious rage, they destroy what you worked so hard at creating.

You would be in shock, wouldn't you? You would be heartbroken.

This is what the Fall amounted to for God: the greatest heartbreak in cosmic history.

The Banishment

In a moment of heartbreak, God banished Adam and Eve from Eden. He took humanity and removed us from his dream.

Peace would be no more. Purpose would disappear. Rejection would reign, all because we chose our dream instead of God's.

With tears in his eyes we were forced out. This was the fall of God's dream.

At this point you may be thinking, "Well, that's awful news." And I would agree with you. The news of the Fall is awful. It's as bad as hearing about an affair from what appeared to be a healthy marriage, or embezzlement from a faithful employee. It's gut-wrenching news, but it doesn't end there.

The Plan

When my wife, Brianne, was 14 years old she began writing letters to me. Once a month she would sit down at the desk she had in her bedroom and she'd write letters to me. Some of the letters were prayers meant to encourage me. Others were notes describing the activities of her day and what she was feeling in the midst of them. But the majority were letters describing things she was dreaming of.

She would dream about what life with me would be like. She would talk about the day we would get married, and what

> *As I read these letters I became so overwhelmed. These were precious dreams. These were priceless promises.*

our wedding day would look like or where we would live, or what kind of activities we would do together. She would even dream about the amount of kids we may have.

They were innocent love letters, and the amazing thing about them is that when Brianne wrote them we didn't know each other.

When she was a young girl, a friend of hers encouraged her to write letters to her future husband as a way of blessing him. So for 10 years she wrote letters to me, without me knowing, and on the day of our wedding, during our first-look photos, she gifted me with these letters.

As I read these letters I became so overwhelmed. These were precious dreams. These were priceless promises.

God's Dream Letters

The Bible is God's dream-filled promise to humanity. It is a story of God's promise, that even in the midst of our rebellion, he will one day bring us back to Eden. And even in the midst of the Fall, in Genesis 3, we are given two glimpses of this promise.

The first is found when God condemns Satan (the serpent) after he manipulates Adam and Eve. God promises Satan judgement by telling him that one day an offspring of Adam and Eve's will "crush his head."

Now, if you grew up in the church, you were likely taught that Jesus is the "offspring" of Adam who crushes Satan's head. That through Jesus' life, death, and resurrection, Satan is crushed and Jesus reigns in victory. That is entirely true.

But what I want you to think about when you read this judgment of Satan in Genesis 3 is how an ancient person, born 4,000 years ago would have read this promise of God.

In ancient culture, when people thought of snakes the first thing that came to mind was evil.

> _Just because God revoked Eden from us doesn't mean he has a Plan B for us._

Snakes instigated death. They killed the innocent. They lived in the dessert. They were creatures that false religions worshipped and thought were blessings from their gods. By every definition, snakes were agents of evil.

So when God tells this serpent—the creature that helped rebel against Eden—that one of their children will crush his head, they would have seen this as a promise to _reverse_ the the Fall. Satan deceived humanity, and if one of their own people kills him, maybe, just maybe, they could return to Eden.

||||||

The second glimpse of God's promise is in verse 24. In that verse we are told that after Adam and Eve are banished from Eden, angelic beings are placed around the Tree of Life in the center of Eden, along with a flaming sword, to ensure that we will never go back to Eden. It's gates are closed. We can't get in.

Have you ever wondered why God never destroyed Eden, but just protected it from us?

He did that because the dream was always Eden.

Just because God revoked the garden from us doesn't mean that he has a Plan B. It doesn't mean that he started over with a new dream, like a entrepreneur who's business failed—an Eden 2.0.

No. His dream for our world has *always* been and *always* will be Eden.

So instead of destroying Eden after the Fall he protects it. He guards it with angelic beings and a flaming sword to ensure that *if* we ever come back, we are there because we belong.[2]

Taken, but Not Gone

Eden may be taken, but it is *not* gone. Humanity has been removed. We've lost the freedom we once had. We've lost holiness we once experienced. We've lost the eternal life we once had. But it is not gone.

One day, our Savior will come. He will come with the power of angels and a flaming sword, and he will crush the serpent. He will return us to where we belong, Eden.

This is the dream of God.

And from Genesis to Revelation we are reminded over and over again, just like I was reminded by Brianne's love letters, that God will never give up on his dream.

Notes:

1 I understand that Genesis 3 is the introductory chapter on the Fall, and some have interpreted the "cool of the day" as a form of judgement on Adam and Eve. But exegetically, one cannot find evidence for that in the text.

The assumption from the story is that God has walked with Adam for quite some time, but realized Adam needed Eve, and thus, provided Eve to Adam. But the truth remained that God dwelt with humanity in Eden long before the Fall ever occurred. This theme of "dwelling with" is also one of the major outcomes of Jesus' death and resurrection. He restored God's "dwelling presence" to his people. Thus, restoring Eden to God's people.

2 In the book of Revelation, one of Jesus's followers is caught up in a vision from God. In this vision he sees God's plan to restore the world back to Eden. And when he sees all of this amazing stuff happening (which we'll talk about in chapter seven), the initiator of this cosmic renewal is a glorified Jesus Christ. And the way that John describes Jesus is incredibly similar to how Eden is being protected. Jesus comes from the cloud, from where he was seated at the throne of God, and as he comes angelic beings are worshiping him (the beings who were meant to guard Eden!), and he has a flaming sword coming out of his mouth. That sounds eerily similar to Genesis 3:24, doesn't it? That's the point. Jesus is the one who brings us back to Eden, which we'll talk about a lot more in the rest of this book.

4

God's Promises of a Garden

A garden requires patient labor and attention. Plants do not grow merely to satisfy ambitions or to fulfill good intentions. They thrive because someone expended effort on them.

LIBERTY HYDE BAILEY

Dreams of Eden

One of the most exciting things about the Bible is that it's a story. It's not a cookbook on spirituality. It's not a dissertation on cosmology. It's not a history book. But it is a story. A grand story of God's dream.

If you're a nerd like me and you love fantasy novels, the Bible is everything you could ever dream of. It's a spellbinding story of power, loss, redemption, love, corruption, and hope. All held together by a promise of good conquering evil. It is the greatest story ever told. And the thing that is so incredible about this story is that once you begin to realize that God's dream has always been Eden, as you read the Bible from cover to cover, you discover that God reminds us of this dream over and over again.

||||||

> _God is a masterful author with an uncanny ability to leave breadcrumbs of his dream of Eden sprinkled throughout the story of the Bible._

I am currently reading a trilogy called _Red Rising_. It's a story about a young man named Darrow who comes from a faction in society that has been oppressed for hundreds of year, and in order for his people to experience freedom he leads an uprising. Darrow systematically infiltrates the highest levels of factions in society and causes a civil war. He does this because he is convinced that when the war is over his people will be freed.

It is an incredible story. And one of the things that I am so impressed with as I have read each book is the amount of breadcrumbs the author places in each book.

In book one Darrow will have a conversation with a friend about a topic that at the time doesn't seem to make any sense. But then, in book three, some 900 pages and two years later, that same conversation will turn out to be one of the most important conversations in the entire trilogy.

The author has the uncanny ability to intertwine the most mundane pieces of information throughout the story. It is an art that very few authors are able to accomplish well.

||||||

This is what God does throughout the Bible. Like a clever author, he alludes to his dream in one story with passing comment from the prophet Moses, then in another story, some 1,000 years later, he boldly proclaims it through the prophet Ezekiel.

God is a masterful author with the uncanny ability to leave breadcrumbs of his dream throughout the story of the Bible. And it is our responsibility to find those breadcrumbs so that we would never lose site of his dream for us.

One of those breadcrumbs is found in Ezekiel 36.

Breadcrumbs of Eden

Everything is destroyed. Homes are burnt to the ground. Businesses are ruined. Neighborhoods are ransacked. Churches have been desecrated. Children weep at the loss of their parents. Parent are cry out. Their children are gone.

Everything is gone.

||||||

This was the scene of Jerusalem after it was conquered by the Babylonians.

For hundreds of years God warned his people that something like this would happen.

When he delivered them from Egypt, he promised them a land just like Eden, called the Promised Land. It was a land full of prosperity, presence, and provision. And when he promised them this land he asked in return for their faithfulness. He didn't want another Fall to occur, so he warned them. He warned them to remain faithful. He warned them to be content with his dream, and in return he would be faithful to them. He would provide for them. He would protect them. But in the midst of his warnings, his people turned from him. Just like Adam and Eve.

When God offered to be their king they said "no" and demanded a human king instead. When God wrote laws for their flourishing they broke them in ignorance. When God requested they worship him and him alone because he was the only true God, they turned to other gods, hoping that they would be like the serpent, promising them their heart's desires.

God's people turned, and after hundreds of years of warning them, God finally broke them.

This is how one prophet described these events:

How deserted lies the city, once so full of people! How like a widow is she, who once was great among the nations! She who was queen among the provinces has now become a slave. Bitterly she weeps at night, tears are on her cheeks. Among all her lovers there is no one to comfort her. All her friends have betrayed her; they have become her enemies. After affliction and harsh labor, Judah has gone into exile. She dwells among the nations; she finds no resting place. All who pursue her have overtaken her in the midst of her distress. The roads to Zion mourn, for no one comes to her appointed festivals. All her gateways are desolate, her priests groan, her young women grieve, and she is in bitter anguish. Her foes have become her masters; her enemies are at ease. The Lord has brought her grief because of her many sins. Her children have gone into exile, captive before the foe. (Lamentations 1:1-5)

It was a season of judgement and the Israelites could do nothing to stop it.

You would think that at this point in the Bible God would give up. That after the Fall, then the flood, then hundreds of years of patiently asking his people to be faithful only to have them turn away, he would give up. He would wipe the slate clean.

But he doesn't.

Instead, during their time of exile, God left breadcrumbs of his dream.

In a surprising act of faithfulness God used the prophet Ezekiel to promise them Eden:

"Therefore say to the house of Israel, 'Thus says the Lord God: It is not for your sake, O house of Israel, that I am about to act, but for the sake of my holy name, which you have profaned among the nations to which you came. I will sanctify my great name, which has been profaned among the nations, and which you have profaned among them; and the nations shall know that I am the Lord, says the Lord God, when through you I display my holiness before their eyes.

I will take you from the nations, and gather you from all the countries, and *bring you into your own land.* I will sprinkle clean water upon you, and *you shall be clean* from all your uncleannesses, and from all your idols I will cleanse you. A new heart I will give you, and a new spirit I will put within you; and I will remove from your body the heart of stone and *give you a heart of flesh.*

I will put my spirit within you, and make you follow my statutes and be careful to observe my ordinances. *Then you shall live in the land that I gave to your ancestors; and you shall be my people, and I will be your God.* I will save you from all your uncleannesses, and I will summon the grain and make it abundant and lay no famine upon you. I will make the fruit of the tree and the produce of the field abundant, *so that you may never again suffer* the disgrace of famine among the nations.

Then you shall remember your evil ways, and your dealings that were not good; and you shall loathe yourselves for your iniquities and your abominable deeds. It is not for your sake that I will act, says the Lord God; let that be known to you. Be ashamed and dismayed for your ways, O house of Israel.

Thus says the Lord God: On the day that I cleanse you from all your iniquities, I will cause the towns to be inhabited, and the waste places shall be rebuilt. The land that was desolate shall be tilled, instead of being the desolation that it was in the sight of all who passed by. And they will say, "This land that was desolate has become like the Garden of Eden; and the waste and desolate and ruined towns are now inhabited and fortified." Then the nations that are left all around you shall know that I, the Lord, have rebuilt the ruined places, and replanted that which was desolate; I, the Lord, have spoken, and I will do it.'" (Ezekiel 36:22-36; emphasis mine.)

I want you to think about what this passage says because it is absolutely amazing!

In a time when Israel had turned from God in ways that seemed almost unimaginable—ways identical to the Fall—God chose to *not* give up on his people. He chose to remain faithful to his dream even when his own people turned for the thousandth time!

In this passage God promises his people that even though they are destroyed, their suffering will not last forever. Their homes have been destroyed and their lives have been uprooted. But it will turn around very soon. He will take what was once *desolate* (something without fruit, without life, without hope) and he will turn it into the *Garden of Eden*. He will take their suffering and he will turn it into joy. He will take their shame and make them the honor of his own name. He will restore them, make them new, and give them new hearts to follow him forever!

In the midst of his people rebelling against him, God's lavishes his dream of Eden upon them.

I don't know about you, but that is something I want so badly for my own life. Newness. Forgiveness. Eternity.

|||||||

"This land that was desolate has become like the Garden of Eden!" (Ezekiel 36:35)

||||||

When I became a Christian at the age of 17, I came to faith out of a lot of brokenness. I had a secret addiction to alcohol and pornography. I struggled with suicide, and my home-life was falling apart. I was a mess, and because I was such a mess, it took a couple of years for my faith to "take hold." It took almost 2 years for me to pray on a regular basis, 3 years to read a book of the Bible all the way through, and 4 years before I experienced freedom from my addictions. It was a difficult first couple of years.

When I was 20 years old, three years into my faith journey, I booked a one-night stay in a prayer center in Colorado Springs. I wanted to dedicate a whole day and night to praying, fasting, and figuring out my faith. So I booked the room.

While I was at the prayer center I began reading the book Ezekiel. At the time I had never read any book in the Old Testament, but I always loved the name Ezekiel, so I started reading, and to be honest with you, I understood almost none of it. I had no idea who Ezekiel was, I didn't know the context of the Babylonian Exile. I had zero framework for understanding 90% of the book, but I kept reading. I kept reading, asking God to speak in the midst of my lack of understanding. Then after about 5 hours I got to chapter 36. The chapter we just read above. And when I read it, it blew my mind.

Here I was, a broken young man trying to know God, and I read these incredible words of hope. Words that promised that God would never give up on me. That despite my failures he would give me a new heart and transform my life forever. That he would, one day soon, restore me and the rest of our world to the Garden of Eden!

That, friend, is the incredible dream of God. That despite our failures he will turn our world into the Garden of Eden.

But How?

At the time of writing this book, my son Ezekiel (I told you I liked that name!) is three years old. He is a blonde-haired, skinny little white boy who loves

Daniel Tiger's Neighborhood, McDonald's chicken nuggets, and baseball.

Now, because Ezekiel is a typical three year old, he is inquisitive. He always wants to know what is happening and why is it happening. Sometimes his inquisitiveness comes across as defiant (a trait I think he learned from me), while other times it is innocent inquiry. But nonetheless, one of his favorite questions is, "How?"

How does that work, Daddy?

How do you blow up a balloon?

How do you pour a bowl of cereal?

How do you pray?

He loves to ask the question, "How?"

When it comes to our own understanding of God making our world like Eden, we have to ask the same question. "How is God going to do that?" The answer is absolutely incredible.

Hidden within this passage is a promise that God will be the one who renews everything, much like he did

> *In order for Eden to be restored a new garden must be planted. And as that new garden begins the old garden must be restored.*

when he created the world in Genesis 1 and 2. It won't be us who cause these dreams to unfold, but it will be God. It will be God's handiwork. And the way that happens is through the gardens of Jesus.

Jesus in the Garden(s)

Throughout each one of the Gospels in the New Testament there is a narrative that is not often seen on the surface. As Mark is writes about the cost of discipleship, as Matthew is writes about Jesus fulfilling the Law, as Luke writes about Jesus saving the lost, and as John writes about the miracles of Jesus, there is hidden story of Jesus in the midst of gardens. Four gardens, to be exact.

You see, what most people don't realize is that in order for Eden to be restored a new garden must be planted. A new creation process must take place. And as that new garden takes shape the old garden must be restored. Seeds must die. The gardener must work again. And that is what Jesus does in the Gospels.

In the Gospels Jesus finds himself in the midst of four different gardens: the Garden of Rebellion, the Garden of Rejection, the Garden of Reconciliation, and the Garden of Restoration. Each of these gardens are allusions to the Garden of Eden and God's dream found in Ezekiel 36, which leads us to rest of this book.

We are going to spend the remainder of our time walking through the four gardens of Jesus together. As we do that we are going to see how, as Jesus walked through each garden, he did with the explicit purpose of bringing us back to the Garden of Eden.

Part II: The Gardens

5

Garden of Rebellion

*It was such a pleasure to sink one's hands into the warm
earth, to feel at one's fingertips the possibilities of the
new season.*

KATE MORTON

New Garden

This last year my wife and I moved into our "forever
home." For the first six years of our marriage, we lived
like crazy nomadic people trying to save for a home.
We payed off $100,000 in student loans. We bought
and sold an apartment and townhome so that we could
make enough money on each for a downpayment on a
new home. We sacrificed a lot, but this year it all payed
off.

We bought a single-family home, with a garage, three bedrooms, a backyard, with beautiful trees and quiet neighbors. Six years ago this home existed only in our dreams. But now, it was ours.

One month after we moved in and finished all the initial move-in projects that come with any home, we set our eyes on our backyard. Previous to house, we never had a backyard, so having a yard where our dog could run around and our sons could act crazy was a gift. Or at least, we thought it was.

The day we set out to work on the yard, my wife walked into the garage as I was getting our lawn mower and said to me, "Josh, I think the previous owners had a garden."

Now, before you think, "Aww man! What a gift! A garden waiting for you! Wow!" I want to stop you right there. My wife didn't come into the garage saying, "The garden of the previous owners is flourishing! There are flowers and delicious vegetables growing as we speak!" No, she said, "I think the previous owners *had* a garden." This meant that in our backyard were planters, and in these planters was an infestation of overgrowth. Where there was once life there was chaos. Weeds were growing everywhere. The soil was miserable. There were no tomatoes, no cucumbers, just weed-like flowers covered in grassy vines, planted in dirt that was dry as bones. There was no life, only the *potential* for it.

So as you can imagine, my first response to Brianne was positive. I didn't want to go through the hard work of replanting a garden. I wanted to destroy it with my lawn mower and move on.

But she insisted! "Josh, I want to plant a garden. I want to see what it can become. I mean, think about it, what if the boys learned how to garden and were able to grow something. Wouldn't that be so beautiful?"

If you are a man who is married with children you know exactly what I did next. I gave in, and we began the hard work of replanting a garden, all because my wife saw the potential of what was once desolate.

The Garden He Enters

Throughout the Bible, we are reminded that our world is not as it should be. Like an overgrown garden, our world is corrupt. Weeds abound. The soil is dry. Life is hanging on by a thread, and yet, throughout the Bible we are also reminded that Jesus came to make it new. Like an eager gardener, ready for the re-working of a barren planter, he comes to bring life. This is why in the Romans 5 Paul talks about how Adam and Eve were the representatives of humanity's fall. They were the culprits of destroying God's dream, but Jesus came as a man, who was greater than Adam and Eve, and through his faithfulness he is bringing our world back to Eden. Jesus' primary mission has always been to be the gardener of God's dream by restoring Eden, and the way that he does it is by entering into the Garden of Rebellion.

||||||

When the Fall occurred in Genesis 3, many theologians classify the garden that Adam and Eve were in as the Garden of Rebellion. In that moment, Eden was ruined and what came from the mistakes of Adam and Eve was _rebellion_. The world as they knew it began to fall into despair. Death entered the world. Corruption took over the hearts of humanity. Despair became the norm for humanity. Rebellion caused destruction, but thankfully, in the life of Jesus, that rebellion was reversed.

In Matthew 27, as Jesus is being crucified on calvary, Matthew tells us in verse 38 that two _rebels_ are crucified with him. These two men had committed atrocious crimes against Rome, worthy of the ultimate punishment, and they are crucified with Christ.

Let me ask you this. Why does Matthew take the time to tells us that these two men were

> _He hung in the middle of our brokenness and took the weight of the curse upon himself. And as he did that, we took one step closer to Eden._

rebels? He could have easily mentioned that two other men were crucified with Jesus and we would have been able to put the pieces together that they were criminals. But instead, he intentionally tells us that these men were _rebells_. Why would he do that? Because Matthew is trying to teach us something profound about the *purpose* of Jesus' death.

Matthew places Jesus in the midst of two *rebels* because he is trying to reveal to us that in Jesus' last moments he became a rebel. Not because did anything sinful or rebellious, but because he was becoming a rebel for people like these men, people like you and me.

In his last moments, Jesus systematically reversed the rebellion of Adam and Eve so that we would no longer be under the curse of their rebellion. And he did it all by affiliating himself with rebells on a cross.

What this Means!

This means that every ounce of what occurred because of Adam and Eve's rebellion is already being reversed.

Think about this, if humanity was cursed because we followed the rebellion of Satan, Jesus has reversed that curse. By becoming a rebel on our behalf, we are now free from the bondage of Satan and we have a new King to follow.

If separation from God was the reward for our rebellion, and Jesus became our rebellion, that means that separation from God is no longer an option for our lives. We are longer far from God but he is infinitely near to us. If sorrow was the outcome of our rebellion, our sorrow how now been turned to joy in Jesus. He has taken the curse, the rebellion, the broken of humanity, and he has reversed it all by the power of his death on a cross. This is what Jesus walking through the Garden of Rebellion on our behalf means for us.

You're No Longer a Rebel!

When I became a Christian one of the things I noticed was the lack of joy that so many other Christians experienced. When I asked them about why they seemed so depressed all the time their answers always seemed to be the same. .

"I am feeling the weight of my sins."

"I am a broken person who needs Jesus. I am not a good person."

"There is nothing *in me* to be joyful about. "

Now, as you read those comments, I am sure you can imagine my response. I puked a little in my mouth. I had no idea Christianity was supposed to be so depressing. It blew my mind! Then I realized one profound truth. All of these Christians were wrong! I'm sorry if that offends you, but it's true! Their understanding of themselves and Jesus was all wrong.

These Christians (most of them growing up in conservative Reformed churches) were taught their

> *We are no longer rebels of God. But we are coming back home. To Eden. The dream of God.*

entire life that they are rebels who will barely make it into heaven, and it is only by the grace of Jesus that they can repent, but in the deepest parts of their souls, they are rebels who got lucky. Nothing more.

Here is the deal guys. That is *not* what the story of Jesus found in the gospels.

In the gospels Jesus says that we are "sheep without a shepherd." He sees us as precious children who are lost—who are corrupted by our own sinful desires. He isn't running out with whip waiting to beat us.

In the gospels Jesus becomes a Rebel-Savior who seeks the lost, heals the broken, clothes the prodigal, and resurrects the broken. He hangs on an cross, walks through the Garden of Rebellion, screaming with his final breathe, "You are no longer rebels!"

Friend, if Jesus became a rebel for you to reverse the curse of the Fall, it is now your privilege to live with utmost joy. You are no longer a rebel of God, but Jesus is bringing you back home to Eden, the dream of God.

6

Garden of Rejection

There is no gardening without humility. Nature is constantly sending even its oldest scholars to the bottom of the class for some egregious blunder.

ALFRED AUSTIN

The Prestige

One of my favorite movies of all time is *The Prestige*. It's about two magicians who spend their entire lives in competition with each other. Through years of battling, turning on each other, and ruining each other's careers, they fight to become the greatest magician in their country with the greatest prestige of all.

In the world of magicians a prestige is the final act of the performance. It is the moment when the magician escapes from unbreakable water-filled case, or runs through a wall of fire unharmed, or catches a bullet with just their bare hands. The prestige is the climax of a show that leaves the crowd suspended in utter disbelief.

In _The Prestige,_ both Robert Angier and Alfred Borden do everything they can to have the best prestige amongst each other.

Robert Angier is a man who's prestige is all about cloning himself from one location and within a couple of seconds appearing in a completely different location, defying the law of physics. In the movie, his act is not based on allusion or "magic" but it is based on science.

Alfred Borden is a man with a similar prestige. He disappears in one location and reappears in another. But unlike Robert, Alfred does not use science to woo his audience. He does not go to effort of cloning himself over and over again. But rather, he has a secret. He has a twin brother.

From the moment they became well known magicians, they lived one life. They married the same women. They shared the same kid. They were two men who lived the life of one man for the sake of their prestige.

The saddest parts of the entire movie is that in Robert's attempt to remove Alfred from the public spotlight he frames him for murder. Robert frames Alfred (the twin) for a murder he does not commit, with the intent of him being sentenced to the death penalty and forgotten about forever. But little does Robert know that Alfred is actually two men living the same life. Robert can get one of the men imprisoned and hung, but in the end, the Alfred everyone knows will still live.

So one of the twins heads to hanging station, and in a moment of beautiful sacrifice, he dies for his brother. He dies an unjust death, and yet, as he dies, his family will never know. They will never know the pain of rejection because his twin brother will live in his place.

Rejection

One of the saddest moments in the entire Bible is the moment Adam and Eve are rejected by God. Up to that moment in history God's dream was realized. He lived with Adam and Eve. Everything was perfect. But then Adam and Eve decided God wasn't enough. They turned from God. Which caused God turn from us.

God's turning away from humanity wasn't an emotionally driven decision. It was a decision

In Eden God rejected humanity. Not because the angels offered him a king-sized candy bar and Gabriel has Justin Timberlake hair, but he rejected humanity because we rejected him.

he made out of honor. The people he created didn't want him. So he turned from them. He told Adam and Eve what their sin would do to their lives. He cursed the serpent for deceiving the couple, and then he walked away.

Rejection is one of the worst feelings in life. I still remember the first time I was rejected by a girl I had a crush on in fourth grade. I thought she was the funniest, most beautiful girl I had ever seen. We sat next to each other in class, and on many occasions I cheated off of her math test. It was like we were meant to be.

One valentines day I wrote her a poem, slid it into her desk with a package of Sweet-Tarts, and waited for her to accept my love. But she rejected me. She told me that she was in love with Zack because he had frosted tips like Justin Timberlake and gave her a king-sized Reese's cup. It was heartbreaking. I had never been rejected until then and it scarred me for the rest of my life.

||||||

In Eden God rejected humanity. Not because the angels offered him a king-sized candy bar and Gabriel had Justin Timberlake frosted-tips, but he rejected humanity because we rejected him. We turned away, dissatisfied of his presence, but thankfully *God never* wanted that to be the end of the story.

Garden of Gethsemane

Hours before the crucifixion of Jesus, he left Jerusalem and went out to the Garden of Gethsemane, which was just a few miles outside the city. And when he went out to the garden, while he was all alone, he prayed to God the Father. He knew that the religious leaders of Jerusalem were going to arrest him and condemn him to calvary. So he cried out. This is how Matthew describes this scene:

> Then Jesus went with his disciples to a place called Gethsemane, and he said to them, "Sit here while I go over there and pray." He took Peter and the two sons of Zebedee along with him, and he began to be sorrowful and troubled. Then he said to them, "My soul is overwhelmed with sorrow to the point of death. Stay here and keep watch with me."
> Going a little farther, he fell with his face to the ground and prayed, "My Father, if it is

possible, may this cup be taken from me. Yet not as I will, but as you will."

Then he returned to his disciples and found them sleeping. "Couldn't you men keep watch with me for one hour?" he asked Peter. "Watch and pray so that you will not fall into temptation. The spirit is willing, but the flesh is weak."

He went away a second time and prayed, "My Father, if it is not possible for this cup to be taken away unless I drink it, may your will be done."

When he came back, he again found them sleeping, because their eyes were heavy. So he left them and went away once more and prayed the third time, saying the same thing.

Then he returned to the disciples and said to them, "Are you still sleeping and resting? Look, the hour has come, and the Son of Man is delivered into the hands of sinners. Rise! Let us go! Here comes my betrayer!" (Matthew 26:36-46)

In Matthew's account of Jesus' arrest there is so much to take in. Knowing that he is about to be arrested, Jesus brings his closest friends to the garden to pray. It is no coincidence that Jesus heads to a garden. He could have gone to the temple or to a local synagogue, but instead he heads to a garden.

As he's in the garden, he asks his friends to protect him in the event that the Jews attempt to arrest him, and while he leaves into a dark corner of the garden he cried out to God. Because of the emotional tole of his upcoming crucifixion, he asks for mercy. He pleads with God to give him the strength to save the world, and in the midst of this anguish-filled prayer, his friends reject him.

Peter and the rest of the disciples fall asleep, which gives Judas an opportunity to sell Jesus' whereabouts to the jewish leaders so they can arrest him. And when they come, the disciples run away in fear. They reject Jesus for their own security.

Have you ever wondered why Jesus had to go through so much rejection leading up to his crucifixion? Because he was taking our rejection upon himself. The Garden of Gethsemane was a microcosm of Jesus reversing the rejection humanity so that we would never be rejected again!

Through Jesus' rejection, we are no longer rejected. Through his brokenness we are no longer broken. Every moment he was abandoned is now a reminder for us that God will never abandon us. Every silver coin that Judas was given as he sold Jesus is now a coin purchasing our freedom—our entrance into Eden. That is the beauty of what Jesus accomplished in the Garden of Gethsemane.

Doubt

One thing many people get uncomfortable with is is the amount of doubt Jesus experienced in Gethsemane. I am not talking about intellectual doubt. Jesus was fully God and fully man. He never doubted the existence or faithfulness of God. But the did wrestle with the plans of God.

I don't know if you've ever seen this in the story, but in Matthew and Luke's accounts of the Garden of Gethsemane, Jesus pleads with God to take away the cup he is about to drink. He asks God to come up with a different plan, and as he is pleading with God he sweats so profusely that it seems like he was sweating drops of blood.[1] He agonized over what was going to take place and he doubted his human capacity to endure it.

Now, you can chalk that up to Jesus' humanity and that we shouldn't dig too deep into it. But I believe his doubt is essential to our salvation.

When Adam and Eve lived in Eden they never once doubted. Not once did they wonder if God was going to provide for them, or if he was going to come through on his promises to care for them. Not even once! But soon after their rebellion they started to freak out. They agonized over the shamefulness of being naked. They doubted the care of God.

Doubt became the marker of rejection.

It's interesting that Jesus experienced those same emotions. The Son of God, the one who initiated the plan of our salvation, doubted. And he did it so that we would _never_ have to.

I am confident that if we lived as if we were in Eden, much of our worries would cease to exist. We would be so confident in God's love for us that those feelings of doubt, despair, broken dreams, and pain would all cease to exist.

"Come to Me"

This is the reason Jesus says to us, "Come to me, all you who are weary and burdened, and I will give you rest." (Matthew 11:28) When we come to him rejection ceases to exist. All doubt and agony dissipates. Because we come to him.

The coolest thing about that quote from Jesus is the word "rest" that he uses. That is the same word used to described what God did after he created Eden in Genesis 2. He *rested*. He looked at what he planted, sat back and rested.

Friend, because Jesus went to the Garden of Rejection you are no longer rejected. Every instance of rejection, agony, and doubt have ceased, and in its place Jesus offers you rest. The kind of rest that can only be found in Eden.

Notes

1 See, Luke 22:44.

7

Garden of Reconciliation

It is only the farmer who faithfully plants seeds in the
spring, who reaps a harvest in the autumn.

B.C. FORBES

It Cannot Hold Him!

Many people do not know this about me but I am a
heavy metal music fan. There is something soothing to
my soul about low-tuned guitars, booming drums, and
men screaming about the destruction of the world. It is
mesmerizing. When I became a Christian in 2007, one
of my favorite things to do on a Friday night was go to
a local music venue and watch up and coming
Christian metal artists.

One day I went with a group of friends to a music
festival where seven bands performed throughout the
entire day. One of the opening bands was a band I had
never heard of called My Epic. I researched their
Myspace account to see what style of metal they were
and I learned that they weren't a metal band at all.
They never screamed. Their guitars weren't tuned to
Satanic-levels. They were normal dudes who played
indie-rock music.

When they started their set they played standard
indie-rock songs. They had good rhythm and clever
melodies, but nothing about them blew me away. That
was until they played the final song in their set. The
song is called "Lower Still" and to this day, it is one of
the most profound songs I have ever heard. It is the
story of Jesus going lower and lower for our salvation,
with it's bridge culminating in his resurrection. I've
included the lyrics below for you to read:

> Look, he's covered in dirt. The blood of his
> mother has mixed with the Earth. And she's
> just a child who's throbbing in pain. From the
> terror of birth by the light of a cave

Now they've laid that small baby where creatures come eat. Like a meal for the swine who have no clue that he is still holding together the world that they see

They don't know just how low he has to go lower still.

Look now he's kneeling he's washing their feet. Though they're all filthy fishermen, traitors and thieves. Now he's pouring his heart out and they're falling asleep. But he has to go lower still

There is greater love to show. Hands to the plow. Further down now. Blood must flow. All these steps are personal. All his shame is ransom. Oh do you see, do you see just how low, he has come? Do you see it now?

No one takes from him what he freely gives away

Beat in his face. Tear the skin off his back. Lower still, lower still. Strip off his clothes. Make him crawl through the streets. Lower still, lower still. Hang him like meat. On a criminal's tree. Lower still, lower still. *Bury his corpse in the Earth. Like a seed, like a seed, like a seed.* Lower still, lower still...

The Earth explodes. She cannot hold him!

And all therein is placed beneath him. And death itself no longer reigns. It cannot keep the ones he gave himself to save and as the universe shatters the darkness dissolves he alone will be honored. We will bathe in his splendor. As all heads bow lower still. All heads bow lower still.[1]

My favorite part of the song is the last line of the chorus into the bridge. "Bury his corpse in the Earth. Like a seed. The Earth explodes. She cannot hold him!" The imagery of Jesus' resurrection as a seed being sprouted in a garden is vivid.

The Garden He Enters

In John chapter 19, John gives us a detail of Jesus' burial that no other gospel talks about. In verse 41 he writes, "At the place where Jesus was crucified, *there was a garden*, and in the garden a new tomb, in which no one had ever been laid." (emphasis mine)

As an author, John loved to take details of Jesus' life and make them theologically significant. In fact, most theologians would argue that John's highest priority in writing his gospel was theological, not just historical. That being said, one of the most underrated theological statements in the gospel of John is the *location* of where Jesus was buried. If you were to read one hundred commentaries on the

> *Jesus' burial wasn't a formality for our salvation. It was another garden he entered on our behalf.*

Gospel of John, only about five of them would discuss the location of the tomb from a theological perspective. The reason for that is simple: the way John describes this garden seems out of place.

The details of Jesus being buried in a garden are so obscure that it is often glossed over by modern day scholars. They don't know what to do with it because many of them miss the theological significance of gardens throughout the Bible.

The Bible is a story of God's overwhelming passion to create and restore the Garden of Eden. He is passionate about Eden and he will do anything it takes to bring humanity back to it. This is what the Bible is all about.

It makes sense why Jesus is buried in a tomb in a garden. Jesus's burial is portrayed by John as a planting of a

An overlooked aspect of gardening is the concept of death.

seed. Jesus' body isn't going into the grave so that it can rot away for three days before he is resurrected by the power of the Holy Spirit He's buried like a seed with the promise that once he rises from the ashes of his defeat, he will flourish into the divine tree that we have all been longing for. The Tree of Life.

Jesus' burial wasn't a formality for our salvation. It was another garden he must enter on our behalf—the Garden of Reconciliation.

The Dying Seed

> Jesus replied, "The hour has come for the Son of Man to be glorified. Very truly I tell you, unless a kernel of wheat falls to the ground and dies, it remains only a single seed. But if it _dies_, it produces many seeds. (John 12:23-24; emphasis mine)

An overlooked aspect of gardening is the concept of death. As a kid helping my mom in the garden, it was all work and no play. We prepared the soil, watered it, removed every weed we found, and once my mom approved the soil for planting, we pushed our little fingers three inches into the ground, placed a seed in the three inch whole, and waited three weeks to realize that we were terrible gardeners and nothing ever "took" in our Colorado climate. It was an unpleasant learning experience. Even when something did grow, whether it was a tomato vine, or a sunflower, it was unpleasant. But even in that unpleasantry I never thought about death. To me a garden meant life. But oh, how I was wrong.

When a seed is planted in the ground to germinate it goes through a re-birth process. It breaks and begins to grow, and in the teachings of Jesus, this process is called the "death of the seed." Now, the seed doesn't actually die, or else it would cease its germination process. But you can understand the death imagery Jesus uses as he speaks of a seed in a garden.

In order for life to flourish in a garden death must take place. There is no such thing as a beautiful garden without a reminder of sacrifice, and in the burial of Jesus we see his sacrifice for us.

Jesus had to die, be buried, and rise from the grave because he was a

> *Jesus took our failures to the grave and is now the Gardener of Eden.*

seed for the dream of God.

The moment he was baptized in the Jordan River he became the representative of all humanity's sin. By being baptized Jesus walked with our sin. He walked through the waters of our oppression. He took every act of rebellion, hatred, and fear, and placed it upon himself, bearing that weight for years. Then on the day of his crucifixion the weight of the world's sin pushed him into the ground. Like the seeds I planted as a child, he was pushed lower and lower, to the point of complete destruction. But like a seed, in his death, there was new life.

When Jesus rose from the grave, he became the Tree of Life we rejected in Eden. All of our sin and shame was left in the soil, never to be unearthed again, and in return we were given new life—an eternity with Jesus, living in a garden of his resurrection.

The New Gardener

My favorite scene in the Gospel of John is the moment when Mary Magdalene arrives at the empty tomb and realizes that Jesus is gone. At first, she freaks out. She thinks someone stole Jesus' body. But then two angels show up and tell her that Jesus is not stolen, but he is alive. But she doesn't believe them.

She turns around. Looking outside the tomb where the garden was she sees a gardener, and she begins to ask him where Jesus' body has been taken. "Please tell me, where is my Savior? Where is Jesus? Did the Romans take him? I need to know!"

In that moment she realizes the gardener is not a gardener at all, but he is Jesus.

The reason why John tells about Mary mistaking Jesus for a gardener is because of what it means for our salvation. Where Adam and Eve failed to cultivate the Garden of Eden Jesus succeeds. Where Adam and Eve chose rebel against the dream of God, Jesus restores.

He is the Tree of Life. He is the New Gardener. And when we put our trust in him, we are given the Edenic life we were created for.

Notes

1 See, http://myepicrock.com/lyrics/yet/

8

Garden of Restoration

The human soul is hungry for beauty; we seek it everywhere - in landscape, music, art, clothes, furniture, gardening, companionship, love, religion, and in ourselves. No one would desire not to be beautiful. When we experience the beautiful, there is a sense of homecoming.

JOHN O'DONOHUE

Children's Story

My wife and I have been thinking a lot about adoption recently. As we've prayed and looked into different agencies, one of our priorities is that we want to adopt a child of color. Brianne and I are both white. Our boys are both white, but a lot of our friends not. In fact, one of my dearest friends is an Ethiopian American. We love diversity and at the core of who we are as people we desire to be a diverse family.

Because of that desire, we have purchased all kinds of books on parenting children of color, racial bias, systemic oppression, Jim Crow laws, and much more. And as we've read these books our sons have read on the topic, too.

We purchased an entire series of Bible story books that emphasize on different skin colors, ethnicities, and cultural backgrounds. In these books, Jesus not white. Moses looks Middle Eastern. Pharaoh looks Egyptian. Throughout these stories the writers encourage the reader to think about ethnicities. They will ask questions like, "What color is Jesus?" or, "What country is Paul from?" These books are amazing tools to teach your children about how God created all peoples from all ethnicities.

The first book in this series is called *God's Very Good Idea*. In the book the author writes about God's dream for the word, how humanity broke that dream, and God's plan to restore that dream through Jesus. It

is an amazing little book of theology, and in the first
eight pages there is this lesson:

In the beginning — in fact, before the
beginning — *God had a very good idea.* It was
even better than solar panels. Better than
Super Soakers. Better than chocolate chip
cookies. Better than color TV. Roller skates.
The X-ray machine. Life rafts. Or even
fireworks.

God's idea was to make people. Lots of
people. Lots of different people. Who would
all enjoy loving him and all enjoying loving
each other.

They would all be made in his image. They
would all be like mirrors, reflecting what God
is like.

Because God is full of love, they would be
full of love, too.

So God got to work. He made a beautiful
world for people to live in. *Then he made a
beautiful world for people to live in.* Then he
made the first people — a man and a woman.
And he said to them: "Be happy. Enjoy loving
me and loving each other. Have a huge family

that will fill the earth and look after the earth
and enjoy the earth.[1]

Within the first eight pages of this book we learn
that before God ever spoke our world into existence he
had a "very good idea." In other words, he had a
dream. It was better than anything we could ever come
up with on our own. That dream was to create a
"beautiful world" for people to live in and flourish in
forever.

This little children's book of creation theology is
talking about God's dream of Eden. It isn't using the
theological language we've used throughout this book.
But the concepts are all the same. God dreamed. God
created. God promised to restore. These are essentials
truths for Christianity.

Paradise

There is this word in ancient Greek called *parádeisos*.
It's a word that has it's roots in the Persian empire
around 600 BCE, when the Persians conquered the
Israelite nation. *Parádeisos* means "paradise," or in

some circumstances "garden," which makes sense if you really think about it. Gardens are places of paradise.

When you scroll through images on Facebook of locations that you would like to vacation, they are usually photos of lush vegetation, streams of beautiful water, and copious amounts of food. We all equate gardens to paradise, and in Greek, there was one word that encompassed that reality: _parádeisos._

Paradise. Garden.

In the New Testament Jesus uses _parádeisos_ two different times. The first time is in Luke 23. In this chapter, Jesus has been condemned by the Romans as a rebel leader and he's made his way to calvary to be crucified. While Jesus hung on the cross, a man who was crucified next to him began to cry out to him. He became convinced that Jesus is the Savior of the world, and just before Jesus died, he says to him, "Jesus, please remember me when you come into your kingdom!"

This man asked Jesus to accept him into heaven when he dies. He believed that Jesus was the one person that could grant him eternal life. So he asks him for a ticket into heaven. "Remember me, and let me into your kingdom."

Jesus' response to him is astonishing. He says, "Truly I tell you, today you will be with me in *paradise*."[2]

He tells this man that he doesn't need to remember him, as if it was going to be a while before these events transpired, but that Jesus would join this man right away in *paradise*.

||||||

The second time Jesus uses *parádeisos* is in the book of Revelation 2. In that chapter, John is given a vision of a glorified Jesus enthroned in heaven. He riding on the clouds of heaven, with a flaming sword coming out of his mouth, and a tattoo on his thigh, with the angels singing behind him "Holy, Holy, Holy." What John sees is pretty awesome! And as he sees this vision, Jesus begins to speak:

> Whoever has ears, let them hear what the Spirit says to the churches. To the one who is victorious, I will give the right to eat from the tree of life, which is in the _paradise of God._[3]

Jesus tells his church that whoever is faithful to him he will grant them the opportunity to eat from the Tree of Life in the _paradise_ of God.

||||||

Here is why Jesus' use of the word _parádeisos_ in these two verses are crucial to what we've been talking about throughout this entire book. When Jesus uses the word _parádeisos_ he is _not_ talking about some place in the sky where cupids fly around while terrible 90's worship music plays for eternity. Instead, both of Jesus' uses of the word *parádeisos* are in reference to what is called the New Heavens and New Earth.

You see, for some weird reason over the past one thousand years Christians have become obsessed with this idea of heaven. We've fantasized about this place in the clouds, where everything will be mind-numbingly blissful. It will be an indescribable place of glory. The key word being *indescribable*.

The problem with that view of heaven is that is that it's not biblical at all. No where in the Bible are there verses that say our eternal resting place will be in heaven. Verses that say that don't exist.

> *That is why Jesus chooses a word that can be translated as "garden" instead of "heaven." His dream has always been a garden.*

What do exist are verses that say that heaven is a spiritual realm of God's presence. It is a place where all humanity *waits* until Christ returns. It is a place where the heavenly beings worship and celebrate the victory of God, but it is *not* the final resting place for you and me.

Our final home, according to the Bible, is called the New Heavens and New Earth. It is our *current world* made new. It is our *current home* completely restored. It is everything we love about world *made new*. That is the place we will live in for eternity, which leads us back to Jesus' use of the word *parádeisos* in Luke and in Revelation.

In both instances, Jesus uses language of a paradise-like garden to describe our eternity with him. He describes it as a beautiful garden, more extravagant that any garden we could ever imagine, that we would live in forever.

I don't know about you, but when I think about that, it blows my mind. This means that *every* aspect of the Fall will be reversed. Our broken relationship with God will be restored. Our suffering will cease. Our lives will be made new. Our world will be fully restored. All because of the victorious power Jesus Christ.

That is why Jesus chooses a word that can be translated as "garden" instead of "heaven." His dream has always been a garden. And there is no greater hope than to know that one day he will restore our entire world to that garden.

Notes

1 God's Very Good Idea: A True Story of God's Delightfully Different Family. (emphasis mine).

2 See, Luke 23:7.

3 Ibid.

Part III: Conclusion

9

Eden For You

If the whole of mankind is to be united into one brotherhood, all obstacles must be removed so that men, all over the surface of the globe, should be as children playing in a garden.

MARIA MONTESSORI

God's Dream

God's dream for our world is Eden. His dream isn't heaven. His dream isn't hell. But it's Eden. A eternity-filled, prosperity-reigning, holiness-experiencing, world-changing garden. That is the dream of God. And because that is his dream, there are very specific experiences Jesus offers to us as he restores our world to Eden.

Purpose

When God created humanity, our primary responsibility was to bear the image of God. In ancient culture, the word *image* meant representative or icon. In that time, when a king owned land one of the things

> *Have you ever felt like everything you did was pointless? That is what it means for us to fracture our image.*

he would do is place statues of himself or items that represented him throughout the land to warn sojourners that that land was his, and he placed those items to remind his own people who their king was. Those statues were known as images.

When God created humanity the primary calling he gave each and every one of us was the responsibility to represent him. We were to represent his authority to the entire world and we were to remind ourselves of who our King was. However, when the Fall occurred, one of the curses of our rebellion was that our _image_ was fractured. Our purpose in representing God became manipulated, and in the end, we lost our eternal purpose.

Have you ever felt like everything you did was pointless? That even when you were accomplishing a task or fulfilling a dream, there was a sense of emptiness? That is what it means for us to fracture our _image._ We've lost our sense of purpose.

But here is where God's dream of Eden begins to change that. Just because we fractured our _image_ it doesn't mean that _we_ are fractured forever. We can still have a purpose. Look at what the Apostle Paul says:

> Now the Lord is the Spirit, and where the Spirit of the Lord is, there is freedom. And we all, who with unveiled faces contemplate the Lord's glory, are being transformed into his image with ever-increasing glory, which comes from the Lord, who is the Spirit... Therefore, if anyone is in Christ, the new creation has

come: The old has gone, the new is here! (2 Corinthians 3:17-18; 5:17; Emphasis mine.)

Even though we fractured our *image* in the Fall, it doesn't mean that is the curse that we carry forever. Jesus took our broken images, and through his resurrection we are transformed into *his* image. This means that even if you don't "feel" it, every thing you do on earth has a purpose. Whether you work as an accountant. Whether you are a doctor. Whether you're a bank teller, car mechanic, sales person, or professional athlete. Every thing you do has purpose. This is the gift that Jesus gives us, and this is the promise of Eden.

No Sorrow

> I saw the Holy City, the new Jerusalem, coming down out of heaven from God, prepared as a bride beautifully dressed for her husband.
> And I heard a loud voice from the throne saying, "Look! God's dwelling place is now among the people, and he will dwell with

them. They will be his people, and God himself will be with them and be their God. 'He will wipe every tear from their eyes. _There will be no more death' or mourning or crying or pain, for the old order of things has passed away._"

He who was seated on the throne said, "I am making everything new!" Then he said, "Write this down, for these words are trustworthy and true."

He said to me: "It is done. I am the Alpha and the Omega, the Beginning and the End. To the thirsty I will give water without cost from the spring of the water of life. Those who are victorious will inherit all this, and I will be their God and they will be my children. (Revelation 21:2-7; emphasis mine)

One of the things that is very common in the Bible is what is called a chiasm. It is when an author will say something in the beginning and end of a section that amplifies the main point found in middle.

A chiasm can look like this:

A (Statement)
   B
      C
         D (Main Point)
      C
   B
A (Statement)

In the above passage from Revelation 21, John is using a chiasm to prove a point. As he talks about the coming of God in the first few verses and as he finishes with what God will say when he does come, he makes a bold declaration in the middle. He says that in the midst of God's presence all of our suffering and sorrow will cease. When he comes, death will be no more, and everything that was part of the "old order" will pass away.

What is amazing about that main point is that John is not just talking about our eternal future with Jesus in the New Heavens and New Earth, but he is talking about what our lives can be like *now*.

You see, the word "dwelling" used in this verse is *skēnōsei*. It is the same word used to describe a tabernacle. In the Old Testament, a tabernacle was a portable building that housed the presence of God. It was a place that could go with the people of God wherever they went to ensure that God would never leave them. And in John 1 we read that when Jesus became human, he *dwelt* with us. John uses the exact same word to describe Jesus' ministry on earth in John 1 and in Revelation 21, and the reason he is doing that is to reveal to us the present promises of Jesus.

Yes, our world is not as it should be. Yes, we will one day die. Yes, we will experience loss. But that does not mean that we do not have hope. Jesus is with us. He has conquered death. And soon enough, we will join him in the New Heavens and New Earth.

Peace for All

One of the curses of the Fall was that Adam and Eve would experience enmity. God told them that because they broke their relationship with him, they would inevitably experience interpersonal conflict. They would begin to fight in ways they never thought possible, and no matter how hard they tried to be at peace, peace would never come.

If you think about it, God promised them war.

From that moment in history onward, every society, kingdom, and relationship has fought against each other. Wars have been lost. Marriages have been torn apart. Enmity has become a marker of humanity.

|||||||

What is so beautiful about God's dream for our world is that God never wanted war to exist. Violence, anger, and hatred are all byproducts of the Fall, and they are all aspect of our world that God has been redeeming ever sense.

Take a look at what John says at the very end of Revelation chapter 21.

> The *nations* will walk by its light, and the kings of the earth will bring their splendor into it. *On no day will its gates ever be shut*, for

there will be no night there. The glory and honor of the nations will be brought into it. Nothing impure will ever enter it, nor will anyone who does what is shameful or deceitful, but only those whose names are written in the Lamb's book of life. (Verses 24-27; emphasis mine)

In these verses John sees one of the final scenes of God's dream for the world. He sees the city of God full of peace. This city has its gates open for every nation to come and go as they please. There is no war. There are no battles for the throne, but everyone lives in harmony together. Can you imagine a world like this?

Can you imagine a world where nations flourish *with* each other? Can you imagine a world where there is no such thing as a mass shooting, or a nuclear warhead, or a destroyed marriage, or a broken relationship? It's hard to believe, but that is the dream of God—a world where peace reigns.

The Dream of God

God's dream has always been one thing: A garden. A beautiful, flourishing garden. It is a dream that many of us have forgotten. It is a dream that many of us have thought was too good to be true.

But it is true.

Every bone is our body aches for it. Every desire of our heart clings to it. Every fiber of our affections hopes in it.

Jesus Christ took the dream of God that was once destroyed by humanity and instead of burning it up and beginning new he restored it.

Garden to garden.

Rebellion to restoration.

He restored it in full. For his fame and for our delight.

This is the garden of God.

This is the dream of God.

THIS IS EDEN

Josh Shaw

Josh is a born and raised Coloradan. He, his wife, and their two sons, Ezekiel and Asher, live in Denver, Colorado. Josh is Pastor of Preaching & Vision at Lighthouse Church.

Josh is the author of both *Spirit-Filled Truth* (2015) and *Eden*. He loves to write, eat chipotle, hang out with his children, and play drums.

If you would like to learn more about Josh, his church, or get in contact with him about anything, please contact him via Lighthouse Church's website at www.lighthousechurch.tv.

If you've been touched by the message of this book and want to help make it available to others, we invite you to…

JOIN THE MISSION!

We believe the message of this book is powerful, and we'd love to put it in the hands of thousands of hungry souls. There are many people in this world—including your own family members, co-workers, pastors, fellow congregation members, and friends—who would greatly benefit from it.

How great would it be for them to read this book with you? Perhaps a small group study of the book would be a great way to share this important message.

JOIN THE MISSION

This book was written with the intention of reaching as many people as possible. With your help, that dream can become a reality.

If you are as excited about the message of this book as we are, you may already have some wonderful ideas as to how you can let others know about it. Here are some other helpful ways you can share this book with others:

Gift a copy to your friends or even strangers.

If you have a website or blog, consider reviewing the book and sharing its wonderful message there. Feel free to refer to our website, also referring back to our website, www.lighthousechurch.tv.

Ask your favorite radio show or podcast to have the author on as a quest. Media people often give more consideration to the requests of their listeners than the press releases of publicists.

JOIN THE MISSION

If you own a shop or business, consider putting a display of these books on your counter to resell to customers.

If you know of any authors, speakers, podcasters, etc., who has access to the wider majority, ask if they would be willing to review a copy on their websites or in newsletters.

Buy a set of books as a gift to someone who would benefit from hearing the message of this book.

Share our website through social media platforms, such as Instagram, Twitter, Facebook, Tumblr, and others.

Thank you so much for **Joining The Mission!**

LIGHTHOUSE CHURCH //
books

8210 W. 10th Ave, Lakewood, CO 80214

Made in the USA
Lexington, KY
03 September 2018